Just One Layup

DEVANTE BLOW

ISBN: 979-8-9910062-0-0 (paperback)
ISBN: 979-8-9910062-1-7 (ebook)
ISBN: 979-8-9910062-2-4 (hardcover)

Ordering Information:

Special discounts are available on quantity purchases by corporations, associations, and others. For details, contact Devante@devanteblow.com

Dedication

Dabriel, everything that I have done up to this point is to make sure that you live the life that you want, not the life that you can "afford." My ceiling will be your floor to build from, I love you and want nothing but the best for you.

- Dad

CONTENTS

INTRODUCTION

Dear Reader,

First and foremost, you are not alone. Whether you're a new agent looking for your way or a seasoned agent trying to bounce back, I was in your shoes once.

I started my real estate journey from the ground up, and it's been tough. Just a few years ago, my bank account was down to pennies, and life sent me a series of really tough challenges. Everything was on the line. That was when I thought about Steph Curry.

Steph Curry will go down as one of the greatest shooters that basketball has ever seen.

But at a key moment in the 2019 playoffs, the Golden State Warriors sharpshooter was having the worst game of his life.

At the end of the first quarter, he had zero points. He missed every shot and picked up two fouls. By the end of the second quarter, he still had zero points.

Curry can usually shoot from half-court and splash it. He can find the net from anywhere on the court. But this game wasn't panning out, and the Houston Rockets took the lead.

Halfway through the third quarter, Curry decided to get back to the basics. Instead of shooting from long range, he started making layups. He stepped away from his typical, flashy three-point shots and focused on the fundamentals.

He'd get a pass or an assist, and then he'd sink yet another layup. Two points and then two points again. Something clicked. He built momentum. After that, he couldn't be stopped.

He went from scoring zero points in the first half to 33 points in the second, which included 23 points in the fourth quarter when the game's outcome was on the line. Many teams fail to score that many points in a single quarter, and this one man did it alone.

He sent the Golden State Warriors to the NBA Finals by going back to the basics.

I also rebounded by getting back down to the basics, and you can, too.

The first eight chapters of this book are about my personal journey. I will walk you through my roots, my beginning as a real estate agent, how I got to where I am today, and all the struggles in between.

The subsequent chapters are about three pillars that changed my game: pregame, game time, and overtime. I'll help you figure out your strengths, find easy wins, and cut back on everything else. We'll make a playbook together so you can systematize your strategy and track your success. I'll help you win.

All throughout, I break down my ideas using sports lingo and jargon. If you're like me and grew up playing or watching sports, this book is for you! It will get you from zero to 33 in your real estate career by getting back to the basics.

Success is yours. All it takes is just one layup!

DeVante Blow

The Struggle

THE DESIRE TO WANT more for yourself can creep up when you least expect it.

It happened to me during my eight years working in the restaurant industry. I liked what I did and was also really good at it. There were customers who came in and knew me by name and some whose orders I could put in before they walked in because I knew their cars. I would have a glass of their favorite chardonnay or pinot grigio waiting at their usual table.

But around year six, I started to feel as if I was just going to a job. I wanted more for myself, though I wasn't exactly sure what more looked like—I had gone as far as I could within my situation. I was going through the motions. The passion wasn't there anymore.

When that happens, you lose the light in your eyes. I never wanted to drop or lower the standards of what I gave to every customer. I also didn't want my inner feelings to reflect onto other people. I thought I was doing a good job of hiding those frustrations and doubts.

But sometimes, people can see us better than we can see ourselves.

I knew there was so much more out there for me, and everyone had their own ideas as to what I should be doing. I constantly heard, "You should be doing this!" or "You should be doing that." After hearing and seeing so many successful people betting on themselves, I started to think maybe I should give it a try, too.

There was one conversation in particular that really hit home. One of my friends from church came in on a busy day.

"Hey, DeVante, you did a great job. But when we walked in and were being seated, we saw you. You had your head down, almost as if you were ashamed of what you were doing," she told me.

As it turns out, I wasn't doing as good of a job of hiding my feelings as I thought I was. And someone else was finally holding up a mirror so I could see it for myself.

This was the moment when I knew the job was killing me on the inside and manifesting itself physically. I knew that it was time for me to go.

Even so, I was overcome with insecurity and fear.

What could I do next? As a creative person, there were so many things that I could do and so many avenues I could take. Instead of quitting my restaurant job right then and there, or giving my two-week notice, I decided to stick with it for *two more years*.

I was petrified. I didn't want to choose just one thing and be pigeonholed. I didn't want to take a leap and wind up failing.

Plus, I liked my routine. My job was a nine-to-five, and I could predict what I was going to make every year. I also knew that if I was going to get another job, it wouldn't be another nine-to-five. To succeed at something else, I would have to bet on myself in some type of entrepreneurship where I would be the product.

I settled for the easy route.

And then the COVID-19 pandemic happened.

It was an awful, awful time. Fortunately, the turmoil of that year helped me to wake up and forced me to take a leap. I left my restaurant job and moved my family to Bellingham—a city six and a half times bigger than our hometown of Oak Harbor. There, I started to explore a new career path in earnest.

In order to find the right career path, I needed to dig deep and figure myself out. This journey took me all the way back to the beginning—back to my childhood and the elements that shaped me.

CHAPTER REFLECTIONS

- Where are you right now in your career path? What is working and what isn't working for you?

- Take a moment to write out a list of three to five people who are honest with you and call you out when you need it. If you don't have anyone in your life like that right now, identify a local organization where you can meet driven, like-minded people.

- What signs in your current career or life situation might be indicating it's time for a change?

- What fears or hesitations are you experiencing that might be holding you back from making a necessary change?

CHAPTER 2

Early Years

GREW UP IN A big family. I'm the oldest (and I'd say the most handsome) of 20 siblings!

My mom had me at 15, but I grew up with my six aunts and uncles who were close in age. One of my aunts is 19 and a half months older than me, and many of them often felt like they were my brothers and sisters—except in this group, I was the youngest. I was sandwiched in between and, in many ways, became a middle child. I grew up getting my uncles' hand-me-downs while I watched my younger brothers and sisters get new clothes. And even though I was the oldest of my siblings, I wound up being the runt. Everyone else is over six feet tall, while I'm 5'10 in my Timberlands!

Despite the numbers, we had so much fun growing up! We could have fun with anything. You throw us outside, and we can find a single rock and be entertained for hours. It was amazing! We didn't grow up poor, but we also didn't grow up rich. We were only inside if the streetlights were on or if we were grounded. That was okay since we hated being inside. We were a family that loved doing all sorts of adventure sports. We rode dirt bikes and went snowboarding, and today, I love going skydiving! We're an adventurous family that loves doing crazy, fun things.

Religion was another component of our upbringing. Some of my earliest memories are of going to church. Our grandparents were pastors, and we spent a lot of time at their house. I played the trumpet and sang in church (which is how I later met my wife!). I even spent seven years as a praise and worship pastor.

Having a relationship with Christ and spreading the gospel are cornerstones of my life. I continue to go to church with my own family today. It's the basis of all our decisions. My approach to a Christ-centered life isn't to shove it down people's throats—it wasn't shoved down mine! I try to live out a Christ-inspired life instead. People sometimes ask me, "What makes you so happy and gives you ambition? What keeps your hope alive?" When I'm asked these questions, I tell them about Christ's love. I believe that living out Christ's mission makes a huge impact and I hope to look back one day to see a trail of amazing humans I've introduced to Christ.

Our large family taught me how to relate to different types of people. I could talk to my Aunt Jerrica, have a big conversation, and be a little vulnerable while we played with Barbies. (I always chose to be the Black Ken doll. Don't judge me!) But I couldn't do the same thing with my Aunt Naomi when she did my hair back (when I had hair). We listened to Usher and Brandy together and bonded over music instead. Being in a large family helped me build relationships. It helped me learn what to do with this person and what to do with that person.

Growing up, there were so many of us that we had this friendly, yet hostile, competitive atmosphere. We could pick on each other, but nobody else from outside could do that. That competitive environment led to what my family really loves: sports.

Sports run in my family. My mom was into track and even trained with world champion Florence Griffith Joyner, who was known affectionately as "Flo-Jo." My mom trained at a young age to run at the collegiate and Olympic levels. My dad was very athletically gifted as well.

Football is the number one sport in my family, though. I played football all the time with my uncles. If they didn't choose different things in life, my uncles could have made it to the NFL.

I joined the football team in high school, and I was *fast*. I played speed positions—corner on defense, going against the other team's wide receivers; kick returner, racing back punts and kickoffs; and slot receiver on offense, which meant I did everything from catching passes and running the ball to blocking.

I loved football, and it taught me to be disciplined.

During my freshman season, my coach told us, "Hey, guys, we're going into football season. You're freshmen, and I want you guys to be in tip-top shape. No more drinking soda."

I brushed it aside. No big deal. I drank a soda that night.

The next day, the coach said, "Raise your hand if you drank soda." I might not have followed the order, but I wasn't going to lie about it. No big deal, right?

My hand shot up along with three other guys.

The coach made us run and do bear crawls until we threw up. If you've ever thrown up soda, the acidity *sucks*. I cut soda cold turkey that day.

While that experience was awful, it showed me the power I have to cut things off in my life. I never drank alcohol, never smoked, and never did drugs. Football taught me the power of cutting stuff off. If you put your mind to it, you can stop or you refuse to start. I know I can choose to be a bigger version of myself.

Football taught me a lot of other things as well. Far more than school, football taught me about life. It taught me how to receive tough feedback. Even today when I get called out, I don't get mad or cry. You can't hurt my feelings. I grew up in sports!

I loved the nitty-gritty of football, the pursuit angles and tactics used to tackle a runner. I gained the ability to read whether someone was going this way or that way. I learned that I didn't need to be the biggest player on the field and that I could succeed if I made smart decisions and played within myself.

I also gained the ability to flip on the switch—to get excited or angry, and to turn it on and go all in and put everything out there when I needed to. That ability to control my emotions continues to serve me today.

Most importantly, it gave me inner drive. It made me realize that this was how I was supposed to approach life, work, and everything else. That was really tough to define before I tested it and put myself out there like that.

One of my biggest learning moments in football was when we won the state football championship in 2006. It was the first (and last) time my school had ever won State. I watched the brotherhood, camaraderie, and the things we had to conquer as a team and individually that led to these moments and helped us win the game we weren't supposed to win.

That year, we didn't add any flashy plays. Instead, we fixed the little things. We reviewed games and practice films. We practiced the basics until they were second nature, and we believed in each other.

My teammates could count on me. "DeVante is playing corner. If they throw it to his side, we know he's going to be in the
right position. We trust and believe in DeVante so we don't have
to try to overcompensate." Of course, we're human, and we mess
up sometimes, but we trusted each other.

We drilled the basics and executed the fine details to perfection. Not only did that make us stronger players, but it built faith
in ourselves and each other.

All that football training and practice gave me a foundation of
hard work—the confidence that if I devoted myself to something,
I could succeed. Being from a big family helped me better tap into
my uniqueness and special talents.

Career success was within my grasp. I just knew it. I just
needed to believe in myself and focus on building good habits.

CHAPTER REFLECTIONS

- Reflect on your life up to this point. What events and which people shaped you most? How do they continue to impact your life now?

- Who are the people you can go to war with and depend on today?

- Be honest with yourself. Do you have the discipline to stop something that is holding you back?

- What activities or experiences from your youth have contributed to your work ethic and character?

- How does your personal background (cultural, religious, etc.) influence your approach to life and career?

CHAPTER 3

Habits and Incremental Success

IT WAS TIME FOR me to move beyond the restaurant field, but I needed more than a career change. I needed a mindset shift and new habits. The first thing I did was write down my goals multiple times a day. When I woke up in the morning, I wrote down what I wanted to be, do, or see in my bank account. When

I went to bed, I'd write them out again.

I put a whiteboard in my room so that I could see my goals. That whiteboard was the beginning of everything that followed. It worked. It showed me where I wanted to go, and from there, I was able to continue to reach for the next thing on the list. It made me hyperfocused on my goals and was my first step down the path of incremental success.

One of the biggest things I wanted at the time was to host a concert. At the time, I was the lead singer and songwriter for a band called DeVante Blow & True Horizon. Every day, I wrote out the goal that we were going to sing at a particular local venue and that there would be a professional videographer at the concert. I was specific about which songs I wanted us to sing.

I was nervous when I made that goal. I had no idea how I would get the money to host a concert in the venue I wanted. Five and a half months later, the venue called *me* and asked if our band would perform. For free. It wouldn't cost me a dime.

As the concert approached, I waited for things to fall apart. My friend, Josiah, was in the military and was told he'd have to move on the day of the concert. Then, *on the day of the concert*, his move date was pushed back. He would be able to perform with us!

Despite my fears, the concert was a huge success. The venue was packed. There was even a professional videographer there. Our band performed at the same venue four more times.

Success took a bit longer for another goal I wrote on my

whiteboard. I wanted to own a Jeep. Not just any Jeep, though. I wanted a blue Grand Cherokee Overland—not the kind that goes off-road, but the fancy one with the bells and whistles that you ride around town. A year and a half later, while in Thailand with my friend, Rodrick (Rod) Rumble, I was on the app Carvana when I saw it. The perfect Grand Cherokee Overland—a vision of blue and chrome. Forget being abroad! I waited until morning in the States, made the call, and worked on a deal. They delivered it to my house and waited for me when I got home.

More than just a focal point, that whiteboard was my first step towards removing limiting beliefs that I had placed on myself. I knew I wanted to make a huge impact. It was bigger than me. I have all these brothers and sisters. People in my family have always said, "DeVante doesn't drink, and he doesn't smoke. If there's one that's going to make it, it's going to be DeVante."

I had heard that for so long and now it was time to believe it, too. Nobody in my family, besides my grandparents, owned a house. Making over $100,000 a year would be great, but nobody believed it was possible. I started to believe I could achieve all these things.

My first habit of writing down my goals paved the way for future habit-building. I still didn't know yet what I wanted to do with my career—that would take me some time to figure out. However, I was establishing good habits, which put me in the right mindset to be successful.

For the first time, I was finally starting to believe in myself and that I could adjust and make the changes I needed to make. I was reminded of that skill during the COVID-19 pandemic when I started to put on the pounds.

Up until 2020, I kept in shape by going up and down the stairs at the restaurant where I worked and playing basketball two or three times a week.

I had a good routine going. And then everything changed.

All of a sudden, I wasn't working at the restaurant. I couldn't go play basketball either. I was more sedentary than I'd ever been in my life as we stayed isolated in the house. As a result of this pandemic, my good habits had been replaced with bad habits.

After that, the little things started to add up. I started to see man-boobs and looked differently in pictures. I weighed almost 230 pounds—the heaviest I've ever been in my life. Things fit differently, too. One day, I was brushing my teeth, and everything was just jiggling. I looked at myself in the mirror and thought, "I can't do this."

It was time to reassess my habits and develop better ones. I started waking up a little earlier every day. When I was waking up early every day, I started walking around to build up my cardio. When I was in the habit of doing that, I added going to the gym and just being there. Then I started working out and got a trainer. Since then, I've been consistent. I've only missed two or three days out of the two years I've been going to the gym. Not only am I feeling great, but I now weigh 190 pounds—down 40 pounds from where I was.

I saw what I needed to do and broke down the steps to get there into the basics.

If I had tried to wake up early and go all out in the gym one morning, I would've failed. That's why so many people fail when they try to make big life changes. They tackle everything at once.

Incremental success through habits will work for you, too. It starts with breaking down what you need to do into the smallest steps possible and then drilling into those habits and routines until they're second nature. Once they're in your muscle memory, you can add another thing. The trick is not to overwhelm yourself with too many things all at once.

I won't lie, though. It took time, months of effort, and dedication to lose the weight. It wasn't an overnight success, but it was a long-lasting success.

Incremental success starts with figuring out how you work best, your habits and routines, strengths and weaknesses. The pathway to success starts with knowing yourself first.

CHAPTER REFLECTIONS

- When have you succeeded against all odds?

- Consider your top three goals and make them clear and precise (e.g., "I want to make over one hundred thousand dollars in the next year").

- Write out your goals somewhere visible at least two times a day, preferably when you first wake up and before you go to sleep. Commit to doing this for the next 30 days. (For extra credit, DM me your goals!)

- What daily habit could you implement to keep your goals at the forefront of your mind?

- What's a recent example of incremental success in your life, and how can you build on it?

- In what area of your life could you apply the principle of small, consistent improvements?

CHAPTER 4

Figuring Out Yourself

AFTER THE COVID-19 PANDEMIC shut down businesses, including the restaurant where I was working, I knew it was time for me to get serious about my next step. But I didn't know where to begin.

I searched on Google and asked around about alternative career options. Around this time, I also found the DISC career assessment and decided to give it a shot. The DISC assessment is a profile test based on four personality traits: drive, influence, support, and clarity. It can be a useful way to determine your strengths and weaknesses and consider what path might lead you to success. The test, which takes 15 minutes, asks dialed-in questions, many of which are repeated with different verbiage.

It gets into your brain and habits. It'll help you understand how you best operate without even thinking. The test will also identify your traits, strengths, weaknesses, and learning style. You can use the DISC assessment results to shorten learning curves for whatever you have to learn—from sports plays to business—and help you implement success.

Here are some of the prompts I answered in my test:

1. Put the terms in order of "most like me" to "least like me": inspiring, introspective, moderate, and strong-willed.

2. Which topic are you most interested in (arranged from first to last)?: The psychology of negotiating to win, creating balance in work and home life, a new breakthrough theory, traditional methods to increase effectiveness, discovering your unique edge, breaking news in market conditions, and a new spirit of volunteering emerges.

3. Arrange from best to worst: a lover's embrace, imprisoning an innocent person, a token of love, poisoning the city water, a technical improvement, justice, a blunder, a telephone, a wreck, a madman, an award for a good deed, a life of adventure, a decoration for bravery, torturing a person, a

foolish thought, prostitution, a short circuit, and a new car.

Based on your answers, the DISC profile will pinpoint your dominant trait or traits, which can then help you understand your best professions and roles. Someone with a high D (dominance) is competitive, results-oriented, and suited for management, while someone with a high C (compliance) is very rules and standards-oriented.

The DISC assessment results were spot on for me. The results showed me as a high influence type, which means I'm a people person and that I do well in front of people. It was also dead accurate in terms of my weaknesses. It told me I'm not the best at detail-oriented work. It hurt my feelings a little bit, but if I'm being honest with myself, it's right. If you give me a stack of papers and I have to read it and write a report, oh God, you're going to be mad at me!

The DISC assessment created a list of suggested career paths for me. The results recommended a career that put me in front of people. First on the list was counselor. My wife is a counselor, so I ruled that one out. Second was life coach, but the uncertainty of the COVID-19 pandemic made this path unappealing at the time. Third on the list of suggested career paths, and the one that resonated with me the most, was real estate agent.

For me, getting the results from my DISC profile was a good time to reflect on my lifestyle and trajectory. I didn't take the results as gospel but instead as a starting point for self-reflection.

Was I happy?

Living the life I want to live and seeing the results I want to see?

It took me three years to fully address my fears and limiting beliefs—I had to dig into and dismantle the beliefs I had about myself and rebuild new beliefs. Seeing my DISC profile helped me figure myself out and dream bigger.

Think about your ideal life in five years. If you're in real estate, perhaps your goal is to make 60 sales a year and earn over $200,000. When you start to envision that life, go deeper. What strengths and qualities do you have that would help people choose to work with you? What makes you special and different from other agents?

Ultimately, quality conversations are the bottom line in real estate. Period. No matter how many houses you're trying to sell, you start with good real estate conversations and try to connect with people every day.

So, if the bottom line is conversations, how do you get to them? It will depend heavily on where you fall on the DISC profile. If you're more of an analytical agent who wants to be in the background and not be seen, you may work best with phone calls. Leverage your tenacity and attention to detail as you reach out to people and track your results. If you're an outgoing and/or direct individual, you should be in front of people. Consider hosting open houses or speaking events and letting your personality shine!

Use the test results to reflect on what the perfect day would look like for you. What feeds your energy? What drains you? How can you change your existing habits and routines to feed your best life and future success?

It will take time to process. Think it through in whatever way works best—whether it's writing in a journal (I have over a dozen pads floating around), talking with someone close to you, talking out loud, or, my personal favorite, driving in silence.

Lean into what you find. That's what I did, and it has made all the difference.

I've recommended that others take a DISC profile, and it's been helpful for them, too. One of the people I suggested a DISC profile to is my best friend, Rod Rumble, who was in the NFL and a military service member. He was looking for a career shift and took the DISC assessment. When he was done taking the test, he called me and said, "Yo, where did you hear about this test?! It's crazy!" The results perfectly described him, too. They helped him identify his strengths and how he operates. He leaned into what he had learned and decided his next steps. Now, he's enrolled in a double master's program in Colorado while he assists Coach Deion Sanders (also known as Coach Prime) and the University of Colorado Buffaloes. He's working with football players and building a cool, new career path.

What could the DISC assessment do for you? What awesome things lay in store?

Put the book down and take the DISC assessment (www.devanteblow.com/disc) for the next 15 minutes. Believe me—it's worth the time. Whether you're secure in your role or seeking a new career, taking an assessment can help you connect with your inner self and align with your core purpose.

CHAPTER REFLECTIONS

- The DISC profile assessment is a valuable tool to find out more about yourself. It divides test takers into four categories: Dominance, Influence, Steadiness, and Conscientiousness.

- Take the DISC assessment and review your results. What resonated with you? What surprised you? What were your strengths and weaknesses?

- Brainstorm a list of income-producing activities that leverage your strengths. Similarly, brainstorm a list of ways to use your strengths to have better conversations with people.

- Write out your perfect day. What do you love to do? What drains your energy?

- Have you taken any personality or strength assessments recently? If not, which ones might be beneficial?

- How well do you understand your natural strengths and weaknesses? How could this knowledge influence your career choices?

- When was the last time you engaged in deep self-reflection about your career path? What insights did you gain?

CHAPTER 5

Jumping into Real Estate

MY DISC RESULTS WERE in the back of my mind when we moved to Bellingham, a mid-sized town located in coastal Washington. I felt like real estate might be a strong fit for both my personality and what I wanted to earn. I met with Tim Cornwall, a managing broker and owner of Bellwether Real Estate. It was a small boutique brokerage with about 30 agents at the time.

We clicked immediately. During a meeting with Tim and

other team members, I was shown what the company had accomplished and asked about my experience in sales. "Well, I come from the restaurant industry," I said after hesitating for a moment.

"Honestly, you'd be surprised how many people come from restaurants and are super successful at real estate!" Tim said, unfazed. I breathed a sigh of relief.

As I quickly learned, real estate was a completely different ballgame than working in the restaurant business, and it came with different qualifications.

Tim told me about the Washington real estate test. In Washington, real estate agents must take a 90-hour course, followed by a two-hour test with over 200 questions. Tim told me that it's not very common for people to pass on the first try. When he told me that, I got a little nervous. I didn't know if I could do it.

As it turned out, my life wasn't in the right place to give the test—and real estate—my all. My wife was still in the military and was on a deployment that had been extended by three months. She was gone for almost a whole year when the base where she was stationed was bombed.

I was freaking out. I wanted my wife home. I couldn't commit to anything fully—mentally or emotionally. It was important to me to be 100% ready before I committed to a new career path.

So I did what lots of people do when they're afraid or aren't ready to take a big step—I disappeared.

I ghosted Tim.

"I can't do it, I can't do it," I thought.

Even after coming to my moment of truth at the restaurant and unlocking my alignment with becoming a real estate agent, I was still afraid.

I was still scared of the potential for failure and coming up short.

Your path to your dream life isn't going to be a direct, straight line, and don't be surprised if you doubt yourself along the way. Part of this process is about reprogramming your self-sabotage tendencies and unlocking new potential within yourself.

Life is always going to be complicated, and if you allow it, it will get in the way of your dreams.

After my wife returned from her deployment, she left the military and started a new career as a social worker.

And I was still stuck in a rut.

My wife and I have these awesome, honest, one-on-one talks—and after she returned home and got settled, I asked her an honest, scary question: "Babe, what was something that you were looking forward to me doing or something you're disappointed in?"

My wife said, "You know what? There was a time when you were really interested in real estate, and you just kind of dropped it. I was really excited to see you try it."

Oh, that hit deep.

Soon after that, I was riding my bike in Bellingham when I passed by the Bellwether Real Estate offices, and I felt convicted. I told them I would join their team and get into real estate, but I ghosted them instead. My grandparents always told me to redeem my word. I owed Tim an apology.

I parked my bike. As I was going up the stairs, I ran into one of the team members who'd interviewed me. She was mad at me because they were so excited about me joining the team. All she said was, "Oh, hey, you," and kept walking. My tail was already between my legs, and I hadn't reached the office yet.

I got to the office upstairs and the receptionist asked, "How may I help you?"

"Hi. Is Mr. Tim here?" I asked, and while I was asking, he came out of his office, cracking up laughing.

"What's up, man? Give me some," he said while bringing me in for a hug.

I dove straight in. I said, "Hey, to be honest with you, I came here to apologize. I want to redeem my word. I told you I was going to join the team, and I went in a different direction."

He said, "Oh, man, it's all good. I forgive you. How's it going?" As Tim started to talk with me about real estate again, I thought back to my DISC profile. I knew I could excel here. This was an opportunity I couldn't pass up twice. It was time for me to shine.

If I could talk my way into this opportunity after leaving Tim high and dry, maybe I would have the skills to convince somebody to trust me to sell their house and to be able to come through.

I took the real estate course over two weeks and passed the exam on the first try.

Boom! All right. Let's get it!

I soaked in the first month of boot camp and thrived on connecting with others. The other realtors provided a lot of support and advice, but there was still a steep learning curve. I was grateful to be a member of the Tim Cornwell Group at Bellwether Real Estate.

Part of the boot camp was actually getting out into the field. Tim took me and four other new real estate agents to an open house to show us how to set it up. As we walked through the house, Tim pointed at things to make sure we knew what we were talking about.

He pointed to a small closet near a bathroom and asked what it was called. "It's a towel closet!" I said confidently.

Everyone started to laugh!

Confused, I asked, "Why is everyone laughing?"

"That's a linen closet!" another person in the group told me.

I never knew that! That was how little I knew about real estate. It ended up taking me a year to learn all the terminology because you just don't know what you don't know!

When someone first asked if they could build an ADU on a property, I was confused. What was an ADU? I didn't lie or bluff with them. If I didn't know, I told people straight up. People know when you're bluffing! I later learned that an ADU was an accessory dwelling unit, kind of like a mother-in-law suite.

I learned a lot from other real estate agents beyond the terminology. While shadowing another real estate agent, he gave me a great tip. When showing a prospective buyer a house, take them to the curb or the end of the driveway and look at the house with them. Ask them, could you see yourself in this house just looking at it from here?

My background in the restaurant industry was not just helpful in learning how to read and understand people—it also helped me during my first open house. To this day, it was the busiest open house I've hosted! I felt like I was working a Saturday night at the restaurant. When I was working as a waiter, I knew the menu front, back, left, right, all the way around. If you asked me a question, even on the fly, I had the answer for you. Even though I've never drank or smoked a day in my life, I knew what we had in the bar and which wine pairs best with a particular meal.

I prep for the open houses the same way. I know the property all the way to the square footage of the lot that it's on. Before the open house, I recited all the specs a couple of different times, just like I did when I was studying the menu.

"There are four beds, two and a half baths on a 1,803 square foot lot. The last time it was listed was twelve years ago for four hundred ninety-nine thousand dollars. There were five different offers, and it sold for five hundred twenty-eight thousand dollars." I even studied the schematics so I knew where the septic tank and everything were.

Despite my preparations before this first open house, the most popular question took me by surprise. "Why are the previous owners moving?" People asked me that again and again throughout the night.

I told them, "I don't know, but give me your name and email, and I'll get you that answer before the end of the night." Now I had their contact information in my client retention management system (CRM), and they had their answer! It was a win for both of us.

There were some disappointments, too. Early on, a potential client said to me, "We're going to buy a house with you," but then signed with someone else. I didn't know that I needed an agreement signed between us yet. That lesson stung.

Another pragmatic lesson I learned was the importance of cell phone reception. During the first three months of real estate, I was going out to the boondocks to show a house and I lost reception. I couldn't access GPS to find the place, so I was 30 minutes late to the showing. Then, because I didn't have cell phone reception, I couldn't access the physical key to show the house. The young lady who was waiting for me to show the house was polite, but she didn't talk to me again. I don't show properties far out like that often anymore, but when I do, I print out the directions

MapQuest style!

There were so many wonderful moments in those first months, too. It was my second sale ever to a couple named Thomas and Rebecca. They were a young, engaged couple looking for their first house during the height of COVID when houses were flying off the market. Every house had multiple offers to beat out.

They really wanted the third house we saw together. It was perfect for them! They'd put in offers on two other houses and we'd been outbid. "Let's be super competitive," I suggested.

It worked. We beat out the offers!

When I heard the news, I FaceTimed them. They were confused when they picked up the phone (I hadn't video-called them before). "Oops," I said, pretending to be embarrassed. "I didn't mean to video call, but since I have you on the phone, I have news about the house. And, well…" I dragged out the moment and looked away, pretending to be sad.

They braced themselves for the bad news.

"You got the house!" I said. Thomas' face went blank in shock as Rebecca went wild in the background. It was the coolest moment to be able to do that for them. A perfect moment I'll never forget.

We've stayed in contact ever since. They're now married with a baby boy, and they're looking to buy their second house.

Around four months into real estate with Bellwether, we (Tim

Cornwell and the other team members) moved to eXp Realty—one of the fastest-growing real estate brokerages globally, with almost 90,000 agents, and it happens to be based in Bellingham. This move opened up more doors and broadened what I could learn.

I was so excited to start selling houses and getting some wins. I was finding my way as a real estate agent! But I still needed to figure out my own process—to unlock what worked best for me. People were giving me lots of advice, but just like in life, there wasn't a one-size-fits-all approach to real estate.

CHAPTER REFLECTIONS

- What are your limiting beliefs? In what ways have you been holding yourself back? Why aren't they gone yet?

- If you could do anything, what would your future look like?

- You can't soar with the eagles while you're chilling on the ground with the chickens. If you're serious about your real estate career, surround yourself with driven entrepreneurs and agents and contact a coaching agency for additional mentorship.

- What skills from your current or previous jobs could transfer to a new career?

- What are some knowledge gaps you need to fill to succeed in your desired field?

- Are you prepared for the initial challenges of a career change? What support systems do you have in place?

You Are the Magic Bullet

STARTING OUT AS A real estate agent is tough.

You are suddenly running a business—one with opportunities, stakes, and ramifications.

People see the lifestyle outcomes for successful agents and expect that it's going to happen for them. Unfortunately, it's not that simple.

This isn't a hobby. To succeed, you need to stay committed to learning and growing.

On the heels of the learning curve come the "magic bullets." The second someone gets their real estate number, everyone and their mother comes with something to sell. I can't tell you how it happens, but it does. Everyone says, "Hey, I got the best leads for you, I've got the best social media plan for you." Or, "I can make you this website, and it's going to make you a millionaire!"

But at the start of my real estate career, I was still feeling my way around Bellingham. I didn't know many people there, so I had to make a lot of phone calls. I had to build my pipeline fast. I was desperate, and it made me (like many rookie real estate agents) weak to the magic-bullet mentality.

I made some early mistakes. I hired a guy to train Filipino virtual assistants to make calls to prospective clients for 40 hours a week. While these assistants did the best they could do, they struggled to connect with people in the U.S. The return on investment was awful. We made one sale from it and it was a $200,000 house. After spending well over $12,000 and six months of effort, I only had a single sale resulting from the virtual assistants. All I wished was that I could get my money back.

I should've had more faith in myself instead!

After the failure with the virtual assistants, I felt defeated. I had to reflect back on what had gotten me into real estate in the first place.

I desperately wanted to be the first person in our family to consistently earn over $100,000. I wanted to break my family's generational poverty mindset.

But that wasn't my biggest "why." The biggest reason I wanted that income was so my son wouldn't have to struggle with the things I struggled with growing up. I didn't want to give him everything, but I did want to give him all the tools he needed to succeed.

Another initial goal of mine was to return to Oak Harbor someday and run for mayor. I shared this goal with Tim Cornwell one day.

"Why do you want to run for mayor?" he asked.

"I want to build a youth sports facility. As a kid, there was nothing to do out there. Give teenagers a whole bunch of time and nothing to do, and you end up with trouble!" I said.

"Why don't you just make a whole bunch of money so you can do what you want without jumping through political hoops?" Tim replied.

That made a lot of sense! My real "why" wasn't to hold political office. I wanted to give back to the community I came from and leave a legacy.

As I considered the scale of my motivations, I knew that I had to build my business. To do that, I needed to build routines that really worked for me.

I didn't want to throw noodles at the wall. I sought out coaching and dialed into my strengths—my charisma and ability to connect with others. I thought about my perfect day and started to build my schedule around that gradually.

For me, my perfect day was to wake up at 5 a.m. and go to the gym. I would then come home, shower, relax, and prepare for the day between 7:30 and 8:30 a.m. My business day would start at 9 a.m. with outreach—whether that's responding to emails or going onto Instagram to engage with local businesses, friends, and clients (and funny fail videos too!). I might also shoot content to upload so I can stay top of mind for people.

I set aside time from 11:30 a.m. to 2:30 p.m. for meetings, either via Zoom or in person. From 2:30 to 5:30 p.m., I would help people get their houses ready for market or showings.

I would become my own magic bullet—the solution to my problems. I would use my unique gifts and strengths to serve my audience and community.

And you can do the same—you are your own magic bullet!

If you've taken the DISC profile test, then you already have an idea about your strengths and weaknesses. Now, it's time to reflect on what is driving you. What is your "why"?

Start by making a list of your goals. Let's say that your goal is to be rich. Take a step back and really explore that goal and your motivation behind it. What is "rich" to you? Let's say it's earning over $100,000 a year. If you want to make $100,000 in a year, why is that? What would you do with it? Perhaps you want to pay off your mom's house so she doesn't have to worry about it.

In that case, $100,000 is great, but the real goal is providing for your mom.

Now, how can you reach that goal? Take stock of your current habits and routines. Then, think about your strengths and weaknesses while you think about your goals, whether it's a perfect career, perfect business, or perfect sports performance. What does that look like for you? What do you have to do to get there?

First, we need to change the little things and build better habits. Stop scrolling on social media. Try to wake up a little bit earlier.

The trick is not to do it all at once. You don't start by waking up early, going to the gym, and getting a hard workout in every day. Just start off by practicing waking up early. Take the first steps and work toward the schedule that will support your goals.

I hope you take the time to really explore these things. It was a good thing I defined my goals and worked on my routines when I did because life was about to get a lot harder.

CHAPTER REFLECTIONS

- A lot of people will try to sell you products that claim to give you real estate success. Ultimately, though, the only magic bullet is YOU.

- Put your biggest and wildest goals where you can see them every day.

- What are your "whys"? What drives and inspires you? Is there an even bigger motivation behind them? Write out your whys and put them where you can see them every day, like in your wallet.

- How can you leverage your strengths to reach your goals?

- Build toward those goals through your habits, leveraging the value of incremental progress. Reflect on your current habits and routines. What is serving you, and what needs to go? Consider which small win you can integrate into your routine and implement it today!

- What unique qualities do you possess that could set you apart in your field?

- Have you ever relied too heavily on external solutions instead of leveraging your own strengths? What was the outcome?

- What are your top three personal and professional goals? Why are these important to you?

CHAPTER 7

Buckling Down

I **WAS HAVING A GREAT** first year in real estate and was learning a lot. I was closing deals. Then, around the summertime, my wife and I were playing basketball when my wife collapsed.

We'd only been playing for five minutes! What's going on? My wife had always been healthy and in shape. We took her to the hospital, and the doctors told my wife that she had pulmonary embolisms throughout her chest.

When they said she was the youngest person they'd ever put on blood thinners, I replied, "I didn't need to hear that, but thank you for the truth, doc!"

How could I still go out, work as the breadwinner, and not be there with my wife when she needs me at the house? It was so hard. It was one of the hardest things I ever had to do.

Fast forward a year after the pulmonary embolisms, and we found a lump in her breast. She went to her doctor. The lump turned out to be stage two breast cancer. All throughout the next year, the fight was now against cancer.

Once again, I struggled with not being at home with my beautiful wife. I was filled with fear and anxiety, and it was compounded by this second major crisis.

What if I was missing out on precious time with her?

Yet I had to be out producing and selling houses. The number one thing you don't want when you have medical issues in your house is financial issues on top of it.

I was struggling to close deals. The real estate market was tough that year. Over 60,000 real estate agents left the market before August, and people said that interest rates would hit 8%.

There were days when we had to be in Seattle, a two-hour drive away, by 5 a.m. for her treatment. These appointments were sporadic but also nonnegotiable.

I was overwhelmed. My time was squeezed to the max and I didn't know how to juggle everything. I slowed down.

There was a moment in early December when I realized I

wasn't selling houses. I had completely lost my momentum. My last closing was in November, and, my God, the bills wouldn't stop!

My wife encouraged me.

"You need to get back out there. I'm going to be alright," she told me.

That's when I knew I needed to get back to the basics.

I looked at my day and cut out all the things that weren't working. I stopped making what felt like 1,000 phone calls a day to people who didn't want to speak to me. This was an energy drainer and an inefficient use of my time.

I instead focused exclusively on what I was naturally drawn to and good at—relationships, making funny videos, and house showings. I reached out more to my sphere of influence, those who knew me personally. I made daily Instagram posts and did open houses. I didn't do anything else but focus on those areas.

I blocked out the negative voices who said the real estate market was crashing or we were heading into a recession. I knew deals were being made. Even if they were harder to come by, they were still out there. Instead, I used my platform to educate people about the real estate market.

Back at home, I had to go back to the basics, too.

As a husband, I felt like there should be more I could do for my wife. There would be nights when she was going to sleep and crying from the pain of chemo. I couldn't take that pain away from her, and it was killing me.

A close friend pointed out to me that I couldn't physically take the pain of cancer away from my wife. No matter how badly I wanted to, I couldn't do anything about it. He suggested I switch my focus from taking her pain away to cultivating a house of peace and joy so that when she came home from chemotherapy, she wouldn't have to worry about those things. She could instead come home, be herself, and let her hair and defenses down.

He was right. I couldn't heal her, but I could give her DeVante. I focused on what made her fall in love with me in the first place—making her laugh!

As a family, we had to work on communication and scheduling. We posted our family calendar on the wall, listing everything from my wife's doctor visits to my open houses. When something major happens, things can spiral out of control if you aren't communicating effectively.

Our faith and church community also helped to ground and comfort us during this time. We kept going to church, singing, and holding on to that faith.

Throughout all of this, I couldn't drop the ball on my own health either. I had to keep going to the gym every morning. It kept me in my rhythm both mentally and physically.

I had to keep my shoulders strong to help carry the extra stress and pressure.

Things soon came together. I found that if you do the right thing for a good two weeks, you'll see solid results in a month or two. If you take two days off, you'll see the results of your laziness in a week! I focused and moved the needle forward on my mental, physical, and professional well-being. Aside from those areas, I was solely dedicated to my family.

The results came fast. In January, I closed on three houses, and by February, I was doing even better. I closed a couple million dollars' worth of houses before we got to spring!

Things only went up from there.

My wife's cancer treatments were successful! Even when she lost her hair, she never lost her smile. She never lost her grace, and that was super important. Even though her treatment culminated in a double mastectomy, she was never a victim of cancer. Today, she continues to be strong and cancer-free.

Meanwhile, I was working fewer hours than I had in previous years but getting far better results. By focusing on what I loved, I had more time with my family and was able to better provide for them. As I tracked my results, I knew I was onto something.

CHAPTER REFLECTIONS

- Reflect on a time when you were under tremendous career and/or personal pressure. What was the situation? How did you recover from that situation?

- Think back to the list of people you wrote out after chapter 1. Are these the same people you could reach out to if you were in a tough life situation? Who else could you reach out to when things get tough? Connect with those people this week to see how they're doing.

- What does getting down to the basics look like for you?

- What personal challenges are you currently facing that could impact your professional life?

- When faced with difficulties, what core activities should you focus on to maintain momentum?

- How can you better balance personal challenges with professional responsibilities?

CHAPTER 8

Developing Your Playbook

WHEN MY TEAM WON the state football championship, our playbook was filled with a handful of super successful plays. We didn't do anything fancy, and there weren't a ton of trick plays or complicated formations. We had six plays that we knew very well. If we woke up from a dead sleep, we could run those plays and be successful.

We found out which plays worked for us and practiced them

to perfection.

When my wife had cancer and the real estate market was in flux, I asked myself, "DeVante, let's look at the previous year of my real estate business. What was that like? What got me the best results?"

The first play in my playbook was an easy one: I knew I needed to be in front of people. In real estate, the best way I could be in front of people is by doing open houses. When I did open houses in the past, they were all very successful. So, the number one play I put into my playbook was open houses.

When I reviewed my efforts over my first few years in real estate, I identified two more activities I excelled at and that had been successful: posting on social media and reaching out to my sphere of influence. Those were also core activities in my playbook, so I put them into action.

When I created my first playbook, I had to cut out a lot of activities because they didn't play to my strengths. I didn't have time to wait, and I didn't have resources left to waste. It was go-time, and I wasn't going to let the dead stuff hold me back.

One of the first activities I removed was cold-calling strangers. That rarely worked for me—it's difficult to create a connection, and it takes too much time and energy. While doing that worked for some people, it didn't work for me at all!

I found that the more selective I was with how I spent my time and the more dedicated I was to my playbook, the better my results were. I worked less but closed far more deals. I enjoyed the time I spent working more, too, because I was doing what I loved!

Now it's your turn to build your own playbook.

Start by focusing on your income-producing activities (IPAs) and dig into the weeds to figure out what works best for you. Review the past six months to a year—treat it like footage from your last game where you can review the plays that worked and the plays that didn't. What did you do that brought the best results? Isolate the key activities so you know precisely what you did. If you have no appointments, no buyer's agreements, and no listing appointments, how will you produce those things right now?

This is also a good time to reflect on your DISC results. Which activities best suited your strengths? How can you leverage your natural gifts? What feeds your energy?

A helpful tool when you're getting going is finding a coach or a mentor. They can help you identify your strongest IPAs and brainstorm strategies. It's particularly helpful to find one who doesn't share your personality type. They can show you your blind spots. It's good to know what exactly your blind spots are—you don't know what you don't know!

As a high I (influence) on the DISC profile, details are my weakness. Once, when talking with a real estate mentor who is high C (clarity), he told me he knew if he called 100 people, 25 people would answer. Of those 25 people who pick up the phone, five of them are likely to have a good conversation with him. Of those five good conversations, two will set up an appointment; of those, he will likely have one sale. So, that real estate agent knows he needs to make about 100 calls to make one sale. If an analytical person hadn't broken it down for me like that, I would've never thought about it!

It is also important to consider your weaknesses. What are your nonproductive activities? What drains your energy?

If it's a weakness, it doesn't go into your playbook.

There's a cap to how much you can improve your weaknesses. In comparison, there's no limit to how great you can make your strengths. Instead of devoting time to improving your weaknesses, you should focus on your strengths and increase your output while outsourcing your weaknesses.

If I were to buy an online assistant service again, I would hire somebody really good at phone calls. All this person would do is make a phone call and set up an appointment. I would then go to the appointment myself. They would only take out a weakness—scheduling—and leave me to do my strength, which is being in front of people.

This is all easier said than done. It can be hard not to want to keep up with and do the same things as everyone else. Comparison is the thief of joy, and what works for somebody else may not work for you. It's important to remember that where a person is today isn't how they started off.

I can look at somebody's Instagram and see that they have

50,000 followers and thousands of comments on their posts. I even see people asking them to sell their houses! Why is no one commenting on my posts? Why aren't people asking me to sell their houses on my posts?

When I started doing this, I self-corrected quickly. I've talked with the people behind accounts like this, and they've told me the truth. It took them several years, and they had a whole marketing company behind their posts. Suddenly, I'm not doing too badly, all things considered.

As I moved into luxury real estate, I started to think about clothing. Perhaps it was time to wear suits and hats to match the polish of the properties I was showing. I wanted to be dressed sharp!

I had to pull myself out of that thinking quickly. First, that's not really me. I dress smart casual or business casual and rarely go all out with my clothing. I wear a necklace my wife gave me two years ago that never leaves my neck, and the only ring I wear is my wedding ring. Second, where I'm at, it's not cute to dress fancy. Bellingham is a hipster love affair! If I walked around decked to the nines, I would be unapproachable to my clientele.

At the end of the day, you can't compare yourself to others. You are the magic bullet, and that should be your main focus. Don't focus on anybody else—just be yourself and your own special brand of magic.

As you hone in, identify three key plays that will go into your playbook every day. These will be your three strongest activities that play on your natural strengths. It may be tempting to add more than three things to your playbook but don't do that starting off. It's best not to put too many ingredients in the soup.

Don't make the ingredients too complicated, either! For now, you have to get down to your basic activities. You're going to practice them until they're second nature. If that's making 800,000 phone calls, then knock out the first three calls. Boom. Even if someone hangs up on you for each of those three calls, you've made them, and you're that much closer to 800,000 calls. If you have a good conversation, but they weren't looking to buy, that's still a win. You had a conversation with somebody! Add them to your CRM to call later and just keep going.

Paper never forgets. Write out your daily playbook so it'll be like the Ten Commandments. You have to do the same thing, or close to it, each time. If you cooked the best spaghetti once but winged the recipe, you won't get the same results next time.

Hold tight and stay focused! We're getting ready to head into the pregame.

CHAPTER REFLECTIONS

- While playing football, my team focused on our best plays until we knew them in our sleep. This is a great strategy, especially when you're the underdog in the game! Review the past six months and see what worked best for you. Identify your three best plays that get the strongest results for you and build on your strengths.

- You can only build on your weaknesses so much. Review your playbook to ensure none of your core plays rely on your weaknesses.

- Comparison is the thief of joy. Not everyone is the same with the same strengths and weaknesses. Is comparison holding you back?

- What is your real estate market like? Are there any plays you think will work better or fill a particular niche in your market?

- Write down your playbook—paper, don't forget!

- What are the top three activities that consistently produce results for you?

- How can you leverage your natural strengths more effectively in your daily work?

- What tasks or activities should you consider delegating or eliminating to focus more on your strengths?

CHAPTER 9

Pregame

BEFORE THE PROS WALK out onto the court, they have a process to prepare for each game.

For many pro athletes, no matter the sport, prep for any game usually starts on Monday, which will likely be a conditioning day to get their bodies into shape. The athletes practice new plays on Tuesdays and Wednesdays. Thursdays might be a walk-through when they practice plays at 50% intensity, but they'll preserve their strength for game day. Throughout the week, they review game film.

These steps help them get mentally and physically ready for the game.

When I played football, Friday was game day. Throughout our state championship journey, our coach would set us all in the locker room before the game and turn off the lights. Talking wasn't allowed at this time. He'd say, "This is time to mentally prepare for the game. Forget about homework. Forget about your girlfriend who didn't show up or who will be watching you on the field tonight. Get it out of your head. Right now, just think about the game."

You could feel the emotion in the room as we got ourselves into the right mindset. I would review what I'd learned and think about my responses. If I knew I was going up against a certain opponent, let's call him Isaac, I'd imagine that I'm on an island, and it's just me and Isaac. I closely examine his stance for tells. He's in a low stance, and his hands are up. All right, boom. I know he's actually going to block me. He wouldn't be running out for a pass. I visualized that on the field. Then I imagined that Isaac's hand was slightly down and his stance was higher—I knew he was going to run a route. I mentally rehearsed how to react to each scenario during those silent locker room moments.

After the silence and lights out, nobody spoke. Then, the coach would put on some intense music, and we pounded on our chests and put on the war paint. One time, I started playing the *Halo* theme (and got into a bit of trouble for it), and afterward, it became a team tradition. It helped to bring the intensity even higher! After that, we went out and did our pregame warm-ups.

By the time we got to the field, I didn't need to consciously think about the game anymore. I could just respond.

As real estate agents and entrepreneurs, we need a similar weekly rhythm to stay sharp. I've divided tasks into similar segments: skill work, conditioning, offensive schemes, defensive schemes, and film review/walk-through. Breaking apart non-game time activities into these areas will help you stay sharp and ahead of the game!

This is set up so that when you're on the court, you can sink the shot.

Skill Work

Some real estate agents stop learning when they get their licenses, and you should work to avoid this. You have to keep learning to stay ahead of the game. Skill work is all about continuing to study market property knowledge and other key skills like how to write up forms.

Look for multiple credible resources as you build these skills. For example, to continue studying forms, your brokerage will likely provide form resources and updates via your MLS service. Be sure to check for other online resources as well. For Washington-based real estate agents, Annie Fitzsimmons, a real estate lawyer (find her YouTube channel at www.youtube.com/@

WashingtonREALTORS), provides walk-throughs of new forms from a lawyer's standpoint. Look for comparable resources that are relevant to your market(s).

In basketball, when it's time to practice skill work, players break out to practice the specific skills. You go to your group and practice the skills you need for your roles. The point guard is the person who brings the ball to the court, so they're going to practice dribbling, action passes, and making sure they have a deep knowledge of the plays. The center will practice boxing out and rebounding the ball and getting the ball back into the hoop. Their main focus is going to be close to the basket.

Similarly, you should also spend time getting even better at your niche (e.g. location, property type, buyer type, etc.). If you spend an hour a day developing your area of focus, you'll be an expert in a year! Whatever your niche is, knowledge is power. Knowledge is confidence. If your niche is a specific area and you know that area front, back, and center, then there's nothing that catches you off guard.

If you're still figuring out your real estate niche, that's okay! It took me three years to find my own niche. Experience will be your best teacher! In the meantime, be sure to continue to develop the core real estate skill work.

Conditioning

Conditioning is the practice part of pregame that will help you stay the course. It's rehearsing how you'll respond to any situation thrown your way, and it's one of the most important things you can do as a real estate agent.

When you get into sales and entrepreneurship, you don't know what to say at first. It's so easy to say the wrong thing. Sales is a psychological process to get somebody to say, "Yes, I want to buy/sell this house with you!"

One helpful conditioning tool is role-playing, which is when real estate agents practice scenarios together. These exercises are essential not only when you're starting out but also as you grow in your real estate career. These sessions should offer plenty of chances to rehearse answers to standard questions (such as interest rates and low credit scores) but should also have plenty of curveballs.

You can even practice this further by asking the person doing exercises with you to throw as many curveballs as they naturally can into the conversation. Curveball questions could include, "My dad told me not to buy a house unless XYZ politician wins the White House," or "I want to buy a house big enough for me and my parents to live in, but it needs to be below four hundred thousand dollars," when the standard house prices in your area are well above $500,000.

What do you say now? The aim of the game is to stay on the

call for as long as possible. The longer you can keep the conversation going, the more likely you are to get to a *yes*.

Practicing your responses in a learning environment with other real estate agents will let you learn how to think on your feet. It'll also prepare you for running into similar questions or scenarios.

Role-playing with other agents helped me develop more effective scripts for prospecting calls. Through brainstorming and experience, we figured out that when you answer with "Hello, is this so-and-so?" (with so-and-so being the prospective client's name, of course), you've already messed up. You've shown them you don't know them. There are 0.2 seconds until that person hangs up.

Instead of asking if the person on the phone is who you want to speak to, my script now says, "Hi, so-and-so!" This creates a pause and interest. The person on the other end of the phone is intrigued. They think, "Who's calling me now? Do I know who this person is?" Then I dive into why I'm calling!

As you role-play and gain more experience in your field, you should also develop scripts. What works? What isn't working? First, focus on making scripts for your most frequent conversations and then develop more. As you develop each script, say it out loud, preferably with another agent, to see how it flows and feels. Does it roll off the tongue?

Developing scripts builds confidence and competence. If you wing it, it'll be impossible to replicate. The aim is to create predictable processes to get predictable results.

Experience helps me edit my scripts. I used to ask, "How are you?" in my prospecting calls. After a few memorable experiences of learning far too much about their lives, I've edited that out of my script. One person told me their cat had just died. I could never call that person again because I will always be associated with the death of her cat!

One more conditioning tool I use is mentally rehearsing the situation I'm about to be in. I run the plays I'll be doing in my mind with three different scenarios so I know exactly how to respond. If I'm driving to an open house, I imagine what I'll do if it's a dead open house. If no one comes in, I'll use that time productively by working on skill work. I imagine what I'll do if it's just moderately busy—I will engage with each person who comes in.

Is the open house the most bananas open house I've ever had? Great! I'll go up to each person when they walk in. I'll say, "Hello, how are you doing? My name is DeVante Blow. What's your name? Are you from around here, or are you out shopping?" I've not only made a connection with them, but now I can also bucket them into categories. If someone responds with, "We live two houses down and we're thinking about selling soon. We're here to get an idea of what's selling," I'm definitely connecting with them. But if a person responds with, "We're just neighbors who've always loved Bob and Sue, and we want to see the inside of the house," that's also great. I'll say, "Hey, feel free to peruse."

And then I'm on to the next person!

Before I show a property, I drive in my car with the radio off. I rarely carpool or give the buyer a ride. I take that time to turn off the radio and clear my mind so I can be focused and in the right mindset for the appointment. I use this time to review the relevant information and imagine all possible scenarios. This is how I get my mental reps in.

Don't wait until you're in the game to think of what to do. Use pre-appointment time to make your plan. For example, on my way to a listing appointment, I'm going over everything I have to know and repeating it over and over in my head. I'm going over to this person's house. This is the neighborhood that it's in. This house hasn't sold since 2016, and since then, there have been 17 houses sold in the neighborhood. What would a routine for you look like?

As I imagine each possibility, I prepare myself to walk in with a winning mindset. People can smell defeat. If you walk in defeated, it'll show in your stature and speech. It's a red flag. When I shake their hand for the first time, I expect them to sign. If it doesn't go my way at the end of the meeting, that's okay! I'm going to learn from this experience. No matter what happens, I'm going to win.

Offensive Schemes

Offensive schemes are your strategies for prospecting new clients to put at the top of your sales funnel. The sales funnel represents a client's journey before using your services. At the top of the sales funnel are people who might be interested—perhaps they searched for houses in your area or clicked *like* on one of your social media posts. At the bottom of the funnel are people who have signed up with you and are ready to purchase.

You always want to be in a professional state of gaining more clients every day through prospecting, marketing, and more. That feeds the top of the funnel!

As you decide your approach to offensive schemes, consider what sets you apart from the other real estate agents in your area. I know there are about 1,200 real estate agents in my area. Why would a client choose me over the other 1,199 real estate agents? I put myself out there on social media so people can get to know me. People know I'm fun but also know I'll tell you how it is. We're going to laugh a lot! I'm a social media guy, so I'm going to post your house online, and it will look great. Finally, they know I will try to sell it in 30 days or less or your money back (joking!). That pitch puts many people at the top of my sales funnel.

Aside from social media like Instagram and YouTube, I also gain potential clients from public events, open houses, and circle prospecting. Circle prospecting is when you call the neighbors of a new listing you posted. I say something along the lines of, "Hey neighbor, I just want to let you know that I went live with John and Betty's house next door. I see you're a neighbor. We expect multiple offers. Would you entertain an offer at 1.3 million if that came to you?" If they're interested, you've got another listing!

Defensive Schemes

Defensive schemes are tactics you'll use to keep the clients you have. I want everyone who knows and trusts me to keep using me forever! This is completely different from a transactional real estate agent. The goal isn't to use people and throw them away.

One defensive scheme that has worked well for me is staying in touch with previous clients via Christmas cards. Thomas and Rebecca kept me in mind because I stayed in touch with them using holiday cards, and I just bought a house with them and sold their prior property. More importantly, we stay involved in each other's lives!

A recent addition to my defensive schemes is client events. These are open forum events where I present on different real estate topics. This keeps me in mind with prior and current clients and also protects them from terrible, predatory real estate practices.

This year, I'm hosting a client event to show appreciation. If someone has used my services, referred me, or is in my CRM, I want them to come and enjoy something that will cost them nothing. I just want them to come and have a good time!

Film Review/Walk-through

As you systematize your processes, keep notes on what works and what doesn't. This will be your film review and walk-through. This can be as simple as looking at your 1099 at the end of the year to see if you made more money or less than the year before. It can be as detailed as a complex Google spreadsheet that tracks your success rates for different techniques and approaches.

Whether you're making time to reflect annually, quarterly, monthly, weekly, or daily, what matters is that you're consistent. The goal is to make a steady income. Which activities produce the most money? Where are you profiting, and where are you losing? Is there something that could be performing better? Perhaps there is something that was a strength at the beginning of the year but isn't working now. Is that still a strength, or is it a weakness? Track your inputs, too, but remember that things like a social media posting might take several months to bear fruit.

In reviewing what's working, it's helpful to seek mentorship and feedback from people with different backgrounds to see how you can improve. You can't see your blind spots. Some agents use the same headshots from 1977. People don't know who they are when they walk into appointments!

Look on the bigger level, too. Has the market shifted? Perhaps where you're sourcing your leads from isn't working. Zillow-sourced leads used to have a significant conversion rate, but those conversion rates have dropped substantially in my area in the past three years. Some teams in my city still pay over $10,000 per month to get Zillow leads even though they aren't producing the same results.

I also routinely review my vendors and processes. While I love my inspector, in 2021 and 2022, we waived all the inspections because it was so hard to get into a house. Now, I use them all the time!

The pregame period is also the time to gain momentum through small wins. One small win is putting key plays from my daily playbook into my calendar. The plays can't get overlooked or moved—they're on the calendar. One thing on my calendar every day is calling between 5 to 10 people I know and trust. No excuses. If I miss that goal because someone wants to do a showing or something, it's easy to track because it's on my calendar.

While a mixture of pregame activities is essential every day, consider focusing certain days on determined pregame activities. For example, while offensive schemes (prospecting strategies) are incorporated throughout the week, I pay extra focus to them on Mondays and Wednesdays: Mondays because I'm reaching out to everyone whose information I captured during open houses, and Wednesdays because my listings go live on Thursdays.

While you're training for a professional sport, it's important to leave time for the body to recuperate. Similarly, you should add time for rest and relaxation so you don't burn out. When I need a rest day, I let my partners know so they can cover for me. If you're a solo agent, have everything forwarded to your assistant so they can handle emergencies. Whatever your situation, you have to follow up quickly. Most people will understand if you take a day off, but make sure you call them back the next day!

Each small, easy win leads to the next win. By building up small wins and routines, you can remind yourself that you are in control and you have the power to make amazing things happen. As you do this, you'll surrender your victim mentality, too. Goodbye to the mindset of "Oh my gosh, why is this happening?" You will control what you can control.

It's the time to cut things out so you can focus. If you haven't already, it's time to cut out activities that no longer serve you. For me, it was cutting out cold calling and door knocking. What will it be for you? Be focused and prepared because we're heading out of the locker room and onto the court!

CHAPTER REFLECTIONS

- There are five types of pregame plays: skill work, conditioning, offensive schemes, defensive schemes, and film review/walk-through.

- Skill work involves studying market properties and developing other key skills. Identify core resources you can use to enhance your existing skills and develop new ones.

- Conditioning involves rehearsing scenarios, both common and tough. If your brokerage doesn't have role-play sessions yet, see if they'll be willing to start hosting them. Before going into a client-facing situation, think through different possibilities and mentally rehearse how you'll react.

- Offensive schemes are strategies for finding new clients. You want to prospect for more clients. Remember that you want clients in all stages of the sales funnel at all times.

- Defensive schemes are strategies for keeping your existing clients. How can you deepen your relationships with the clients you have? Is there another service you can offer existing clients to help you stand out?

- Film review/walk-through involves regularly reviewing your pregame and postgame plays. How often will you review your progress, and how? Think about how you can track your progress.

- Choose a pregame theme for each day of the week, such as conditioning on Mondays. Make sure it fits your personal and local rhythms. This doesn't mean you won't incorporate any other plays from the other categories (you should always be looking for more clients!).

- Put your playbook and your pregame activities into your calendar. Cut out all extraneous activities possible so you can focus on winning!

- Each small win will lead to another small win. Focus on these wins and controlling what you can control while cutting out what doesn't serve you.

- How can you incorporate skill development, conditioning, offensive strategies, defensive strategies, and performance review into your weekly routine?

- What mental rehearsal techniques could you use to prepare for important meetings or presentations?

- How can you better track and review your progress towards your goals?

CHAPTER 10

Tip-Off— Game Time

THE WHISTLE BLOWS. YOU'VE done the hard work learning your strengths, thinking critically about leveraging them for success, developing your daily playbook, and getting into the right mindset.

It's game time! You're starting to do those income-producing activities, so it's time to put your playbook into action. You're going to run plays that will generate success. You need to stay focused.

The key with your daily plays is repetition, repetition, repetition. Run your core plays until they become second nature. As mentioned previously, one of my key plays was posting on social media. I put that on my calendar and practiced doing it until I didn't have to think about it anymore. After that, I added speaking engagements to my core playbook and then event sponsorships. Each built on my strengths and didn't take away from my initial core plays.

Your three core baseline plays aren't going to be all-encompassing. There will be times when you're out in the field: you're in front of a client, you start making outbound calls, you have a listing or buyer's agent appointment, or you're writing an offer.

In my office, we have a checklist for almost everything. If you get a new listing, there's a 60-point checklist of things to do. If you have a buyer's appointment, there's a list of things to do from start to finish. These checklists help new agents who've never done it before get set and ready to go.

Even though I'm now a seasoned agent, I use the same principle. I've developed playbooks for activities like open houses tailored to my strengths and experiences. For my open-house playbook, I arrive at least an hour early. I go through all the rooms, turn the lights on, ensure everything is nice, and set up the signs. I put myself into the visitors' shoes and identify at least one interesting feature to note to prospective buyers later, like an en suite bathroom.

When legit prospective buyers are done looking at the house,

I ask them how this house compares to the house they're looking for. They go to dreamland and tell me they'd love a house like this one but with another room and a bigger backyard. This allows me to say, "Do you have a minute? I can search for a house that has bigger square footage and footprint if that's something you're interested in." Five minutes later, we've found a property that better fits their search. I can ask if they'd like to check out the house and schedule an appointment to see it with them in the next few days.

Just as with your baseline playbook, plays that work for others may not work for you. One open house action recommended to me was to knock on the doors of all the surrounding neighbors of the house you're showing. While I like the sound of that idea, I won't do it! It's not for me.

An information-gathering play is one type of play that needs to be in all your specific game-time playbooks. An information-gathering tactic in my listing playbook is having a 15 to 30-minute pre-listing interview. These pre-listing phone calls help me dial into the listing estimate by asking about upgrades and other factors that may impact the price of the house. They also let me get to the personalities of the people who are listing. Are they more analytical or emotionally based? How can I connect with them? It allows me to learn why they want to sell, which is both useful to know and helps inform my approach. Perhaps one of the owners received orders from the military to move to a new duty station, and they're sad to leave. If so, I need to tread a little lightly.

This was helpful for one listing I worked on for a friend. She was super excited about the move. She'd fallen in love with a military guy, and they were moving to the East Coast. The mom, who was involved in the sale, was sad because her daughter and grandchildren were moving away. She was heavily involved in their lives. When I talked with the daughter, I shared in her excitement, but I didn't get carried away because I knew her mom, who was with her, was grieving.

This play also helps me understand what I'll need to do to educate the clients. I want to enable them to decide when to list the house and what the asking price will be. I walk them through the realities of their house and the price they can expect. Yes, they may want to sell the house for $500,000, but $470,000 may be realistic, so I don't have a listing out there for over a year.

After running plays, it's important to reflect back on them. What worked? What didn't work? Finesse the plays. See if there is a different sequence that can change the results. In my seller-meeting playbook, I invite them to talk with me at the table instead of taking a tour of the house. If I let them take me on the tour first, it feels, psychologically, like they're still in control. I want to establish myself. I take control by saying, "If you don't mind, I would love to start this presentation by sitting down at the table so I can introduce myself and give you an idea of what to expect from me."

After my presentation, I say, "Hey, you know what? We're getting to the point where I hone in on what I think we should list your house at, but before we do that, would you mind giving me a tour?" I continue to guide our meeting while also building rapport.

Don't be stringent on your plays. When the situation calls for it, be open to calling an audible. Sometimes, you have to make adjustments mid-game. Just because I have a template doesn't mean I stick to it and not adapt. We work very hard to have the opportunity to meet with people in their homes, so don't mess it up by being in your own way. If the seller is really excited about something about the house during a seller's meeting, I'll say, "Not a problem! Let's check it out!" I match their energy!

There may be a day when one of your plays or an audible doesn't work as you'd planned, but that's why you have multiple plays. But no matter what, you have to keep playing when you're in the game.

If you see an opportunity, don't be afraid to pounce on it.

One day, while I was relaxing in bed and looking at for-sale-by-owners' listings online, one of them stood out to me. "That's a nice one," I thought to myself. "That'd be nice to have."

I got out of bed and took my wife with me to view this property and meet the owner in person. I started to talk with him about his pain points. I asked him, "Why do you think this beautiful house hasn't sold yet?"

He replied, "Not enough eyeballs on the property."

As I got to know him, he told me that his wife and daughter had already moved to Texas. All he had to do was sell the house so he could join them, which he was struggling to do in between 12-hour shifts. While he was in the dream state, thinking about moving to be with his family, I said, "Would you find value in me listing this house for you so you can rest more? I'll have eyes on this property and get it sold for you."

I listened to my gut, and it's good that I did! He signed with me the next day. That improvised play propelled me into the luxury market. I was the only agent to get a million-dollar listing in our team's first year of real estate.

You may not know the right play to run. I didn't know what play to run when I got to his house—I didn't have a play. I just went with it and concentrated on the core values of relationships and adding value.

One of the best things about improvised plays, or immediate, imperfect actions, is that you gain experience. If I get a similar opportunity again, I know what to do. I'm more seasoned than the person who's waiting for the perfect moment to take the perfect shot that never comes.

Don't spend too long gathering information before acting. You can get stuck in analysis paralysis and information overload. If you think long, you think wrong!

As you follow your playbook and make improvised plays, you'll find you get luckier the harder you work. In those moments, keep your momentum. In basketball, when you get in the groove, there's something called a heat check. It's when you hit the shot and then another, so you try to take a shot that is of a higher degree of difficulty. If you hit that, you're flowing!

I recently took a heat check. I had a few listings I was working on closing when a few of my previous clients (Thomas and Rebecca, whom I mentioned Facetiming in chapter 5) reached out to me.

They said, "Hey, DeVante! How's it going? Thank you so much for the Christmas card! We're actually driving around Ferndale. We saw your new listing, and we'd love to check that out. Would you have time to show it to us?"

I showed them the house, and they loved it! It's going extremely well, so I decided to go for it. I asked, "Would you like me to sell your current house, too?" to which they immediately replied, "Yes!"

I went for the heat check. I said, "You know what? It looks like you guys want to buy this house. Would you be willing to work with me?" And yes, they did! I was now doing three transactions in one—the seller's new home, the home Thomas and Rebecca chose to buy (the seller's previous home), and the house they were selling. Boom!

In those moments, a heat check can be your immediate action. You've been making your calls and posting online when you think, "Why don't I go live on Instagram today?" Just go for it! Keep up your momentum by taking some smart, calculated risks.

Just remember that whether things are going heat-check

fantastic or are sluggish, you've got to keep your head in the game. When I'm in an appointment, I shut the phone off and concentrate on the task at hand. There is only one phone call that I'll take at all times. My wife can call me—since she knows I'm in an appointment, she won't call me at those times unless it's something important.

Outside of that, the caller can leave a message because I'm in the game. I don't care if I parked incorrectly or what someone said to me yesterday. I'm on an island with this appointment!

It's important to keep focused and playing because life has a way of getting intense. That's when you know you're heading into overtime.

CHAPTER REFLECTIONS

- The key to success with your basic plays is repetition, repetition, repetition. Put your playbook into action! Focus on your three core plays until they become second nature.

- Start developing a playbook for your top income-producing activity. Leverage the resources you already have available (e.g. checklists from your brokerage), as well as your experiences. Make sure there is one information-gathering type play in each specific playbook.

- Are you locked in analysis paralysis? Which areas of your life could benefit from immediate, imperfect actions?

- Lean into a series of successes to go for the heat check.

- Stay in the game if you're in a heat-check moment or if things are sluggish. Stick with your routines and drill into the basics.

- What core activities should you be repeating consistently to improve your performance?

- How can you better recognize and capitalize on unexpected opportunities in your field?

- What strategies can you implement to stay focused during important meetings or tasks?

CHAPTER 11

Overtime

EVERYTHING COMES DOWN TO this moment.

One mistake can cost you that listing. One mistake can cost you that pending in a multiple offer situation. One mistake can cost you the buyer. You're supposed to be done, but you're still going.

You're mentally and emotionally tired.

What are you going to do?

On my football team's journey to the state championship, we

played a competitive school from Seattle. We were the underdogs and locked in triple overtime. It was a cold and rainy December game. We were exhausted and battling through various bumps and bruises and injuries, but we had a deep desire to win. It was on all our faces—every teammate and every coach.

It was fourth down, and we were on the 20-yard line following a penalty. We needed a touchdown to win.

The final play.

It felt like slow motion. The quarterback dropped back. My best friend, Rod, was playing wide receiver. He ran along the sidelines toward the end zone. The quarterback threw the ball.

Rod saw the ball coming and dove horizontally.

Somehow, some way, he caught it for a touchdown.

We rushed the field. We won the game!

I've had my fair share of overtime periods since that high school game. One of those first overtime moments in real estate came soon after my wife began to suffer from pulmonary embolisms. It was the first time someone so close to me had been affected by a significant illness like that, and it really messed with my mind. From August to January, I didn't sell anything. I was down to the last $50 in my bank account, and I spent $40 of it taking a potential client to lunch.

I was terrified. I had a family to support, and my wife was dealing with serious health issues. A lot was going on. I kept thinking of the supposed 87% failure rate within five years for real estate agents that's often referenced online. I didn't want to be part of the 87%.

I conferred with the other real estate agents I worked with, and their responses clarified things for me. They said, "You're one of the best people out there. Just go and get a sale."

It's just that simple, right? They called me to the carpet, which is exactly what I needed. If they can all make it, then I can, too.

I knew I could be my own magic bullet. I reflected back on my strengths and went back to the basics.

The very first thing I did was go back to my online leads and redouble my efforts in open houses. I called people who'd expressed interest in buying within the past year and hammered the phone. I prioritized staying genuine, confident, and knowledgeable. I focused on knowing the answers to common and complex questions that buyers and sellers would have.

Two weeks of hard work in real estate and you'll see the results in a month. Two days of slacking off and you'll see the results in two weeks. As I called the prospective leads, I left voicemail after voicemail. I kept at it because I knew I needed to keep putting in the hours to see the results of my efforts.

That was when I got a call back from a young lady and her father. They were interested in seeing a house! Nobody ever called me back from a voicemail, but that's when I knew I was building momentum.

Stick with your playbook now more than ever. You're exhausted, but your plays should make you feel great at the end of the day. Remember, there's a cap to how much you can improve your weaknesses, but there's no limit to how high you can build up your strengths.

Remembering my "why" kept me going. This was bigger than me. This was about supporting my family. This was about my legacy and the sports center I want to build someday. This was about showing my family that we should make at least $100,000 a year.

I continued to write out my goals three times a day. If anything, it became even more important. It's the power of noticing things. If you think about red cars, you'll see 45 red cars next time you drive. As I kept my mind on my goals, my mind started to see avenues and ways to achieve those goals. Three times a day, I wrote out my goals before I went to bed, after I woke up, and at the office—and it kept me accountable to them.

Keep writing out your goals. Maybe it's time to show your goals to somebody else. Take a picture and shoot it to your best friend. Say, "These are the things that I'm committed to doing." It'll take you a step closer to owning it.

Just as you stay focused on your goals, you also have to stay focused on showing up authentically. You can only hide who you are for a little while, and then the truth will start to appear. There's a thing called "commission breath" in real estate, which is when people sense your desperation for a sale. It's as if you've ceased to be a real person and are a robot real estate agent!

This is fatal because, at the end of the day, real estate is about relationships. I avoided this trap by focusing on the people. I continued to ask, "How can I add value to you? How can I make your day better?" It didn't have to be about real estate. Maybe a friend of mine was having a down day, so I made a funny little video of myself to help them laugh. I fed my soul and theirs this way!

Keep leading with your true self. Short money is short-lived. Long money is in relationships—you can only cultivate those relationships by being authentic, even when your back is against the wall.

Even when things are difficult, you can't stop taking care of yourself. For me, that looks like going to the gym for an hour every other day. Hammer down on your routines because otherwise, you'll fall apart physically and emotionally, and that will seep into everything else.

It's also important to stay in mental shape. This involves checking in with my best friends like Rod and Josiah. They are pillars in my personal life. It doesn't matter if things are good, bad, or indifferent. I can check in with them, and they'll celebrate the crazy wins and lift me up when things aren't going well. Even when the situations are outside their experiences, like when my wife got cancer, they continue to give me sound advice and keep me motivated when I need it.

Even when one mistake can cost everything, you have to keep doing what you know will work. At the end of the day, though, you're (probably) a human, just like I am. Mistakes will inevitably happen. When you do the wrong thing, you have to recover quickly. Data dump fast so you don't bring that mistake into the next play or game. If you can't forget, you'll hesitate and lose. Own it, learn from it, make amends, and move on. Fail fast!

Progress is more important than perfection. If I had waited for the perfect script and perfect scenario, I probably would still only have $50 to my name. You can't quit playing the game because you dropped the ball! This isn't the time to second-guess yourself. You have to move on to the next play.

When you're in the thick of it, it's important to remember all the work that has gotten you this far. On our high school football state championship journey, we'd worked our butts off all week, all season, all year to get to that point. What, in the grand scheme of things, is an extra 10 minutes of overtime?

That 10 extra minutes of extreme effort made all the difference for us. I'll always have that state championship ring. Our faces are still on a banner in our high school. If I had given up on real estate when I got down to my last $50, I wouldn't have found the success that I did or be writing this book right now.

Keep running your best plays. Don't get all fancy and do something stupid! That's when turnovers happen, and you can't afford that right now. That will lead to more mistakes. It's better and more efficient to keep things simple and do what you know will work. Don't try anything fancy. Just stick to the playbook.

What will a bit more effort and time do for you if you stay

focused and keep with it?

There are definitive moments when you know in your bones that you've won and were able to overcome adversity.

When that adrenaline wears off, you're probably going to crash. I don't think I've ever slept so well as when I turned things around. Catch up on rest, but whatever you do, don't lose momentum because that isn't the only battle you'll have to fight.

You did it. Good job! Celebrate! Rest a bit, recover, and then keep it going. Use your confidence and keep moving… but don't forget your playbook!

CHAPTER REFLECTIONS

- You'll know you're in an overtime period when one mistake can cause you to lose the game. Are you in overtime right now? What do you need to win the game? Don't become one of many who give up on realty before you can succeed!

- If you're in an overtime period, get down to the basics. Go back to your core playbook and stick with those key plays.

- Keep writing out your goals. This is the most important time to keep them in front of you.

- Your grit and resilience are of utmost importance. Build a routine that prioritizes mental, physical, and emotional well-being. You can't let yourself go even when you're being pushed to the max at work.

- Even though this is a high-stakes time, you have to let mistakes roll off your back. Mistakes will happen, but you have to stay in the game. Put in another 10 minutes of hard effort. You got this!

- How can you prioritize relationships and add value to others now? Don't get too fancy, but stay at the forefront of people's minds. Stay authentic as you do so. Remember, you are the magic bullet.

- What would an "overtime" period look like in your career or personal life?

- What strategies can you develop now to help you push through future challenging times?

- How can you ensure you're showing up authentically, even under high-pressure situations?

CONCLUSION

Dear Reader,

If you're on the ropes and thinking about quitting real estate, or if you're just starting out, I've been where you're at. Real estate is tough. It requires focus and a lot of hard work. Stay in the game. There are ways for you to be successful. You have to resist the one-size-fits-all mantra that plagues this industry and make plays and a playbook specific to *you*.

If you're looking for further coaching, DM me! (My contact information can be found at the back of the book.) My team and I are ready to send you the assist you need. We will work on mindset first. We'll find those easy, daily wins—even if it's as simple as making your bed. Then, we will hammer down on pregame,

game time, and overtime. We're going to get you ready for real estate success in every moment and every phase, all of it tailored uniquely for you. We will get the win, get momentum, and create predictable, winning results.

Most importantly, lead with authenticity and get back to the basics. The world is waiting for you to win—you're your own magic bullet.

You got this! The game is yours. Remember, all you need is JUST ONE LAYUP!

–DeVante

ACKNOWLEDGEMENTS

I would like to thank the following people who have helped me during my journey:

- Mindy Price
- Tim Cornwell
- Alvera Blow
- My father, Chris Blow
- My mother, Lynette Jenkins
- All of my clients who have trusted me along the way

CREATING YOUR PERSONAL
PLAYBOOK FOR SUCCESS

Step 1: Identify Your Strengths

→ **Take a DISC assessment or similar personality test**

My results: _______________________________________

→ **Ask trusted colleagues or mentors what they see as your key strengths**

Colleague 1: _______________________________________

Colleague 2: _______________________________________

Colleague 3: _______________________________________

→ **List your top 5 successes and identify common factors**

1. _______________________________________

2. _______________________________________

3. _______________________________________

4. _______________________________________

5. _______________________________________

→ **Common factors:** _______________________________________

Step 2: **Review Past Performance**

→ Analyze your performance data from the last 12 months

Key insights: _______________________________________

→ List your top 5 most successful projects or deals

1. _______________________________________

2. _______________________________________

3. _______________________________________

4. _______________________________________

5. _______________________________________

→ Identify common elements in your least successful ventures

Common elements: ___________________________

____

____

STEP 3: **Focus On Income-Producing Activities (IPAs)**

→ Track and categorize your activities for one week

IPAs: _______________________________________

Non-IPAs: _______________________________________

→ **Calculate the ROI of your top 5 activities**

1. _____________________ ROI: _____________________

2. _____________________ ROI: _____________________

3. _____________________ ROI: _____________________

4. _____________________ ROI: _____________________

5. _____________________ ROI: _____________________

→ **List activities that directly led to your biggest successes**

____

____

STEP 4: Choose Core Plays

→ **List your top 5 strengths and top 5 most successful activities**

Strengths:	Successful Activities
1. _____________________	1. _____________________
2. _____________________	2. _____________________
3. _____________________	3. _____________________
4. _____________________	4. _____________________
5. _____________________	5. _____________________

→ **Identify where these lists overlap**

Overlapping areas: _____________________

____

→ **Select your 3 core plays that combine strengths and results**

1. ____
2. ____
3. ____

STEP 5: Develop Specific Playbooks

→ **List the most common scenarios you encounter in your work**

1. ____
2. ____
3. ____

→ **For each scenario, outline a step-by-step process**

Scenario 1: _______________________________________

Steps: ____

Scenario 2: _______________________________________

Steps: ____

Scenario 3: _______________________________________

Steps: ____

→ **Include contingency plans for potential obstacles**

Obstacle 1: _______________________________

Plan: _______________________________

Obstacle 2: _______________________________

Plan: _______________________________

STEP 6: Include Information-Gathering Tactics

→ **Develop key questions for each common scenario**

Scenario 1: _______________________________

Questions: _______________________________

Scenario 2: _______________________________

Questions: _______________________________

→ **Create a system for organizing and accessing gathered information**

My system: _______________________________

→ **Practice active listening techniques**

Techniques to focus on: _______________________________

STEP 7: Practice And Refine

→ **Set aside dedicated time each week to practice your plays**

Practice schedule: ______________________________

→ **Seek feedback from mentors or colleagues**

Feedback received: ______________________________

→ **Regularly assess which aspects of your plays need refinement**

Areas for improvement: ______________________________

STEP 8: Incorporate Pregame Activities

→ **Schedule specific times for:**

Skill work: ______________________________

Conditioning: ______________________________

Offensive strategies: ______________________________

Defensive strategies: ______________________________

→ **Develop a routine for reviewing your performance**

My review routine: ______________________________

→ **Create a balanced weekly schedule**

WEEKLY SCHEDULE

	MON	TUE	WED	THU	FRI	SAT	SUN
6:00							
7:00							
8:00							
9:00							
10:00							
11:00							
12:00							
1:00							
2:00							
3:00							
4:00							
5:00							
6:00							
7:00							
8:00							
9:00							
10:00							

STEP 9: Stay Flexible

→ **Identify potential scenarios requiring deviation from standard plays**

- ____

- ____

- ____

→ **Practice quick decision-making in hypothetical situations**

Situation 1: _______________________________________

Decision: ____

Situation 2: _______________________________________

Decision: ____

→ **Regularly review industry trends**

Key trends to watch: _______________________________

____

STEP 10: Regularly Review And Update

→ **Schedule monthly and quarterly reviews**

Monthly review date: _______________________________

Quarterly review date: _____________________________

→ **Track the success rate of different plays**

Play 1: _________________ Success rate: _________________

Play 2: _________________ Success rate: _________________

Play 3: _________________ Success rate: _________________

→ **Identify plays to remove or replace**

Plays to adjust: _______________________________________

____

STEP 11: Focus On Repetition

→ **Identify which plays need the most practice**

1. ____

2. ____

3. ____

→ **Set daily or weekly targets for repeating core plays**

Daily target: ____

Weekly target: ____

→ **Use visualization techniques to mentally rehearse your plays**

Visualization method: __________________________________

STEP 12: Tailor To Your Personality

→ Reflect on which activities energize or drain you

Energizing: ______________________________

Draining: ______________________________

→ Consider how your personality type influences client approach

My approach: ______________________________

→ Adapt industry best practices to fit your personal style

Adaptations: ______________________________

____

FINAL REFLECTION:

→ What are the most important insights you've gained from this Playbook?

____

____

→ How will you implement these insights in your daily work?

____

____

→ Next full review date:

____

TAKE THE NEXT STEP TOWARD TRANSFORMING YOUR BUSINESS
and reigniting your passion

Join DeVante's email list to be part of a community that's ready to support and uplift you on your journey to success at **devanteblow.com**

Order special bulk purchases for your company, organization, or community at **devanteblow.com**

Book DeVante for speaking and consultations at **devanteblow.com**

CONNECT WITH DeVANTE

Facebook: DeVante Blow - Bellingham Wa Real Estate

Instagram: @devanteblow

TikTok: @devanteblow

LinkedIn: devante-blow

THANK YOU FOR READING!

Thank you for reading! If you enjoyed *Just One Layup*, please leave a review on Goodreads or on the retailer site where you purchased this book.